The Amazing Adventures of Allen and Zorbi

Written by Nuclear Eyes
Ilustrated by Katy Kat

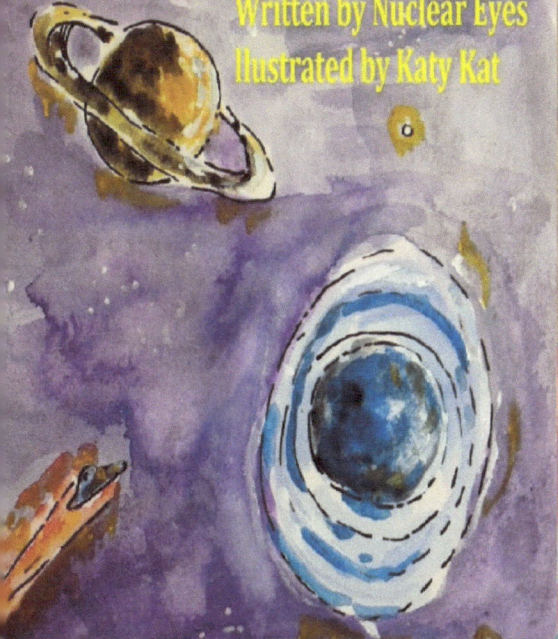

When a small boy from the city moves to the country, all Allen wants is to find a friend to explore the forest with. When what looks like a shooting star zooms across the sky, Allen makes his wish.

Zorbi, an alien being from another planet also wants to explore Planet Earth. When his ship gets hit by a meteor, he too gets his wish for someone to help him discover new creatures.

STARLIGHTS AND SNOWFLAKES

A CHILDRENS BOOK BASED ON THE LAW OF ATTRACTION

A SELF-HELP Book For Kids and Adults

The Amazing Adventures of
Allen and Zorbi

Written by Nuclear Eyes
Illustrated by Katy Kat

Awaken INK

FROM THE CITY : TO THE COUNTRY

The Lucas family had moved from busy New York City, to the calm countryside. The family was now surrounded by trees and wildlife.

Allen, was Mr. and Mrs. Lucas' only child. Allen was really missing his friends and his old Public School in New York City. In the country, there wasn't another house for miles. Allen began to miss the way of city life he was used to. He was feeling lonely. Allen wanted a friend.

Allen's father was raised with a country lifestyle when he was a boy. Mr. Lucas now wanted the same all natural experience for his family.

Although Allen was sad because he had moved away from his friends, Allen's mother and Father grew very happy with their new home in the countryside. They loved the fresh air, the green scenery, and the abundance of life that grew all around them. As a talented gardener Mrs. Lucas was excited about just putting up her greenhouse that protected all her plants while they grew until they could be strong enough to be placed in the outside garden.

*At night, the family sat around their first campfire together. Brilliant stars lit the cosmos. Allen saw how the country skies revealed twice as many stars than that of the skies above the big city.

"So Allen, how do you like living at camp every day? Fun stuff right?" Said Father.

"I miss my friends Dad. I don't know anybody out here*! *I wish I had someone to explore the forest with*," replied Allen.

"You start school next week; you will have lots of time for making friends then. Focus on getting familiar with the land around here. Maybe you can build a fort somewhere?"

"Well, maybe." Said Allen thinking aloud about a construction… "*I wish I had a friend to explore this forest with*, so we could find the best place to make a treehouse! That would be stellar awesome!"

"Patience my dear," said Mother. "All in good time."

"Why can we see so many stars?" asked Allen. "We never saw this many stars when we lived in the city."

"There is not allot of street lights or pollution in the country." Explained Father. "In the city there is smog and other kinds of pollution that prevent the stars from shining through. However, here in the country the skies have more oxygen because there are more trees to make fresh, clean air. Here in the countryside, we are able to see crystal-clear skies that better reveal the star-shine*."

*Suddenly! A shooting star lit up the sky!
It was the brightest meteorite the family had ever seen!*

* == ==== -------- - -

"Make a Wish Allen," said Mom.
"I wish I had a friend to explore the forest with,"
said Allen silently. . .

To the family's surprise the shooting star did not
burn up in the atmosphere as predicted. Instead, the
Unidentified Flying Object streaked across the sky,
getting brighter and brighter until a smoky orange tail
appeared!

The strange burning vessel got lower and lower to
the earth. Blazing over treetops; crashing into the
forest behind the Lucas family home!

"Wow! Was that an actual meteorite landing?"
Asked Mother.

"It looks like something from outer-space just
landed in our back yard!" said Father.

"Let's go look for it!" said Allen excitedly.

The family went through the forest in search of
the UFO.

"Look! That's where the smoke is coming from!"
announced Father.

"There it is! It looks like a giant metallic Frisbee!"
said Mother.

"Cooool!" cheered Allen. "A flying saucer!"

A green and purple figure emerged from the round space-craft; making a way through the billowing smoke. . .

"Stand back!" Warned Father, prepared to protect the family from what looked like an alien creature!

The creature finally came from through the smoke, coughing about. "Greetings Earthlings, my name is Zorbi. I come in peace. I am here to explore your world's ecosystems, to discover new creatures, and learn as much as I can. Are you helpful and friendly humans?"

"Wow! My wish came true!" Cheered Allen. "A friend I can explore the forest with!" Allen ran up to the alien giving him a big hug, grateful for his prayer being answered.

"Allen, no, stay back!" Shouted Father.

"Get away from that thing!" warned Mother.

"It's ok Mom and Dad, didn't you hear him speak?" He's a friendly Alien. "Don't be afraid."

"What is your name, humanoid?" Asked Zorbi the Alien.

"My name is Allen, and this is my Mother and Father."

"I have studied humans. I can tell you are smart for your age. Thank you for being so peaceful and friendly, Allen. I do hope you will show me around?"

After seeing Allen and the Alien hug, Allen's parents were no longer afraid of the Alien. The family grew more curious to why Zorbi was here.

"You are wondering why I am here and where I am from," concluded the Alien after reading their minds.

"I am Zorbi, a celestial scientist from a star system in a far distant galaxy; far away from what you call your *solar system*. I was exploring your planet when a meteor struck my ship! I landed the best I could, and well; here I am."

"I am an explorer too!" started Allen with enthusiasm. "We can explore the forest together! We can both learn a lot from each other! Let me introduce you to the creatures of Earth!"

"That sounds wonderful!" said Zorbi happily.

Zorbi and the Lucas family walked back to the house and sat around the fire place.

"What a beautiful mini-solar-system you have here," said Zorbi looking at the fire he sat around.

"I never thought of a fireplace as a mini solar system before," laughed Allen.

"The fire place is where your human civilization has come from," said Zorbi. "It started with storytelling, cooking, gathering around the fire, exchanging ideas, insights, and you gradually developed a language. Your technology evolved from this hearth."

"Interesting," pondered Father.

"Earth is a fine place to call home," said Mother. "You will like it here. There are many kinds of animals, plants, and creatures that thrive out here in the countryside; and the forest is right behind us!"

"I have always wanted to see this planet's outstanding gardens," Explained Zorbi. "This world is known throughout the galaxy for its beautiful forests and wondrous creatures. You earthlings put on quite a show for us space viewers."

"I would love to see what kind of planet you call home," said Allen.

"We're just glad you're okay after that fall," interrupted Mother.

"I can't wait to show you around!" said Allen with excitement. "Tomorrow morning we explore the forest! Then maybe we can build a fort!"

"I am ever so excited to see what kind of creatures and habitats are on this Planet!" said Zorbi. "I am here to learn as much about this solar system as I possibly can."

"That's a great goal!" said Father. "We are happy to help you in whatever way we can."

The next day the Zorbi and Allen explored the forest together, their hearts both set on adventure and discovery.

Allen and Zorbi approached their first ecosystem. They found four fish inside a small lake.
"SPLASH! BLOP," made the sounds of the fish, catching bugs in the air, landing back in the pond.

Two excited explorers continued deeper into the forest. Soon found was a bullfrog beside a marshy pond; searching for bugs in the tall wet grass.

"RRRIIIBBBIT," greeted the bullfrog.

As Allen and Zorbi walked along the river, they found busy beavers building a dam.

"CRUNCH CRUNCH," nibbled the beavers chewing timber.

The river lead Allen and Zorbi to a rough rocky mountain.
The two explorers climbed to the very top!
Here they found bats living inside a cave.

"EEEK! SQUEAK!" Screeched the sleepy bats.

When the two explorers came out of the cave, they saw a golden eagle flying in and out of the high clouds.

"SCRAAAAAAWE!" called the eagle.

Allen and Zorbi climbed up a tree and found a dove keeping its eggs warm inside a nest.

"COOOUUU," sang the dove to her eggs. "Bird houses have the best views," said Zorbi. "I'd like to build a home like this bird, because it's the same shape as my spaceship."

Allen and Zorbi looked down a hole; to their surprise! Out popped a mole!
"SCRATCH SCRATCH, SCRATCH," dug the mole as it scurried back to the safety of his hole.

When Allen and Zorbi walked down into a deep valley they found a fox sleeping comfortably in its den. The Fox didn't make a sound. . .

When walking along a forest trail, Allen and Zorbi
found a curious owl watching them from the edge of a
tree-branch. The owl had never seen anything like
Zorbi before. "WHOOOOOO?" Hooted the curious Owl.

Allen and Zorbi found a bee on a flower that lead them to a bee hive.

"BUZZZZZZZZZ," flew the many busy bees inside the hive; gathering pollen to make their honey combs.

"There are so many creatures with so many different kinds of homes," said Zorbi in amazement. "Each makes their own unique sound. Each has their own way of life. You can learn so much from observing the nature of this magnificent Planet!"

"Let's build our own ecosystem!" suggested Allen.

Finally, the two friends decided to build a tree house for themselves. With extraordinary teamwork, they had it up in no time.

"The best homes for me around Earth are the ones people make," concluded Zorbi.

The two explorers came back to the Lucas family home, after a long day of exploring and building.

"What an amazing day!" Said Zorbi. "I have learned so much from this beautiful Planet called Earth! This was a super great and highly successful exploration! I have so many good stories to bring back to my home Planet! We have very different kinds of animals, creatures, plants and forests where I am from. Perhaps I will bring you and your family there one day?

Thanks again Allen for introducing me to these remarkable ecosystems, habitats, and creatures."

Many on my home Planet "Orb Z" said I should be afraid of humans, but after meeting you and your family; I believe Earthlings are both peaceful and intelligent after all! Eventually, all of humanity will accept all Life in the Universe, as Family."

"We make a great team!" said Allen. "You Zorbi, are the best friend an explorer could ask for!"

    Zorbi spent the following night repairing his spacecraft until it was fixed and fit for space-travel again.

    Every once in a while, he would look to the stars and imagine what other worlds he could explore next. . .

"My Spaceship is working!" announced Zorbi. "Now it is my turn to show you around! For helping me discover so many creatures on your planet, I want to offer you a journey."

"What do you mean?" asked Allen curiously.

"I would like to return the favor and take you on an adventure study of the planets that orbit your star-system!"

"Really? Of-course! Let's go right now!"

*After Allen got his parents' permission, the explorers hiked back to the space craft.

"Countdown until we are out of Earth's atmosphere!" began Zorbi. "Lets' start backwards from 10."

"10-9- 8- 7- 6- 5- 4- 3- 2- 1= Blast-off! Here we go! Up-up and a-way!"

"Waaaahooooo!" yelled Allen.

"Look!" pointed Zorbi out the window." It's the planet Mercury, the closest planet to your Sun."

"Wow," said Allen. "The Sun looks so big and bright from here!"

"We can't stay here for too long, because we are so close to the sun; this space-craft will get too hot! Let's move on to the next planet."

"It feels like we are driving in a giant Frisbee," laughed Allen. "I thought the stars in the country looked amazing, but here in outer space; they look far bigger and brighter!"

"Look at this one!" pointed Zorbi. "Venus is the 2nd planet from the sun. It's also known as the hottest planet in your solar system because of all the volcanoes and gases all around it. Venus is about the same size of Earth."

"Your right Zorbi," agreed Allen. "Let's get out of here, I'm starting to sweat just thinking about it."

Earth is the next planet from the Sun, but I think you already know lots about the one you live on."

"Mars is the 4th planet from the sun", informed Zorbi. "Mars has two moons, and like Earth it too has polar icecaps."

"Wow! The Circle of Life, isn't just on Earth; it's orbiting everywhere around the stars of the Universe!"

"You are a smart one Allen," smiled Zorbi. "We have so much to learn from each other."

"Over here my friend, take a look on my ship's computer screen: ==========================➔

*Here is a map of this solar system.

The next planet coming up is Jupiter! The 5th planet from the Sun, just past the asteroid belt (a giant ring of space rocks orbiting around the Sun).

Now we are moving towards the outer planets that are much farther away from the Sun. Jupiter is the largest of all planets circling around your star-system!"

"Wow, what a giant sphere!" said Allen.

Saturn is the sixth planet from the Sun. It's the one with the large halo ring around it. Like Jupiter, it has a lot of moons orbiting around it, sixteen in fact!"

"16 Moons!? That's allot!" said Allen.

"The next planet is Uranus, the seventh planet from your Sun. Uranus has a big ring around it too, but this ring is placed up and down from top to bottom, rather than side to side like Saturn's rings."

"Every planet is so different form each other," said Allen. "But each one is a circular-sphere."

"Our solar system is amazing!" said Allen. "Are there other solar systems like this one?"

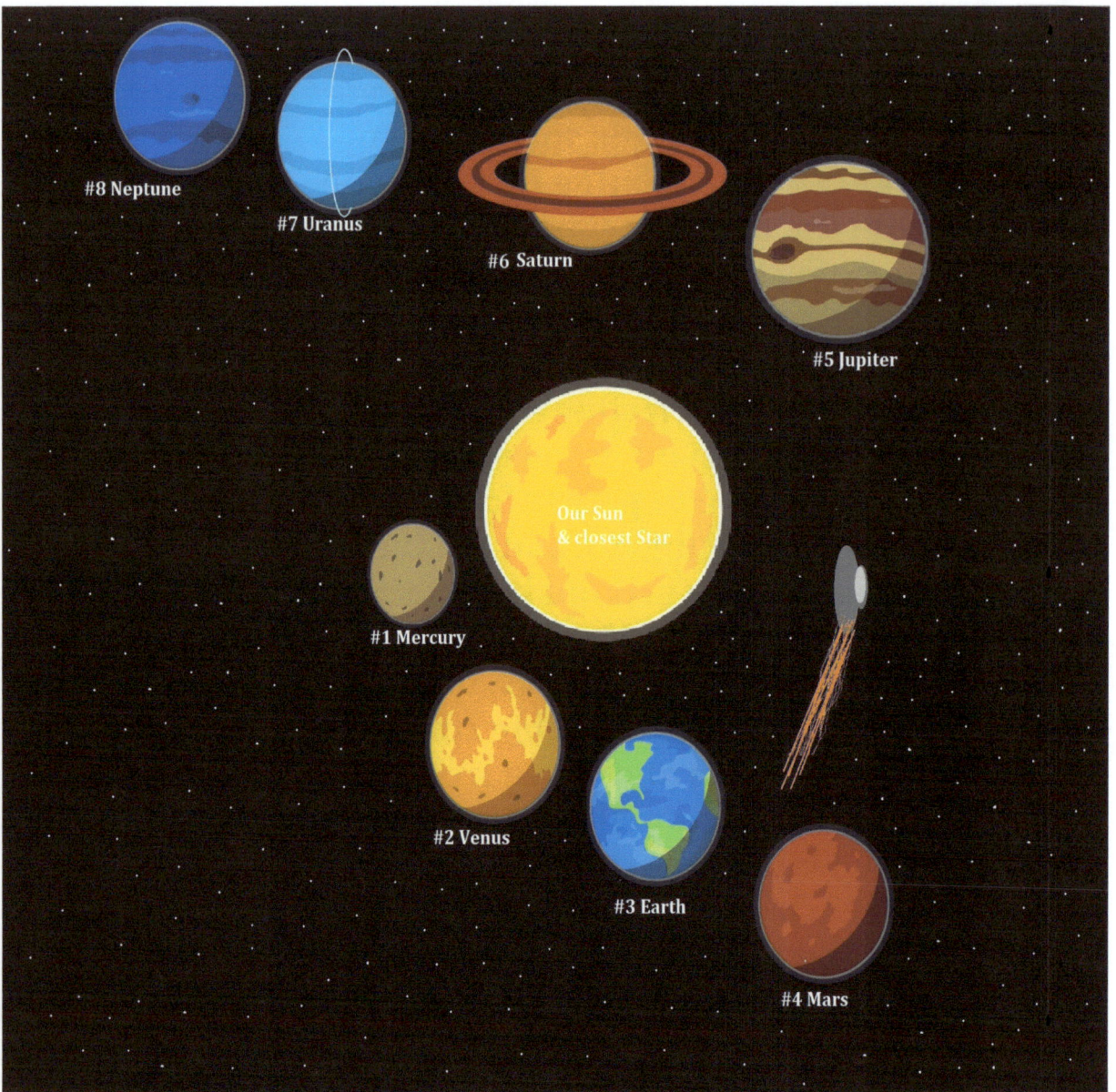

#8 Neptune

#7 Uranus

#6 Saturn

#5 Jupiter

Our Sun
& closest Star

#1 Mercury

#2 Venus

#3 Earth

#4 Mars

"Of course. There are millions, billions, and trillions of solar systems! All of them orbit around stars. But each solar system is unique, complete with its own set of planets, moons, and asteroids."

"Space is amazing!" cheered Allen. "There is so much to learn and explore!"

"Very true," said Zorbi. "But there is plenty of unique things to learn on Earth too. You still have much to learn on your own planet before humanity is ready to visit other worlds with highly intelligent life."

"Neptune is the eighth and farthest planet in your Solar System. There are many asteroids, large mountainous rocks, and other interesting things orbiting your Sun, such as a Planetoid called Pluto. A planetoid is a large mass in outer space, yet too small to be considered a planet."

This Planetoid you call Pluto has an orbit very far from your sun. We are now very far away from the sun's light. It is very, very cold out here! Let's fly back towards the Sun where it's warmer."
"It's time to go back to Earth Allen," announced Zorbi. "Maybe we can explore more of the planets, or even visit another star system next time?"

"I would love that!" said Allen with a growing love and appreciation for the stars.

"Maybe you can show me your home planet next time you visit Earth? I would love to see where you grew up Zorbi! "Orb Z" is it?

"Absolutely said Zorbi. I will see if its ok with my parents if you can come over. You would love *Orb Z!"

*The ship accelerated as it turned back to Earth; zipping past meteors, comets, planets, until landing safely again on Earth.

"You have become my best friend Zorbi," said Allen. He was sad to see Zorbi go. "Come back and visit soon! You are welcome here anytime!"

"Of course I will come back to visit! We still have so much of the cosmos to explore! The universe is forever expanding and creating! There will always be an infinite number of things to learn and grow from."

"Drive safe good buddy!" said Allen. "Watch out for shooting stars and meteors! Because the wishes you ask for, just might come true!"

"I'm going to tell everyone how great Earthlings are!
Fair well Best Friend!"

Also by Nuclear Eyes & Published by Awaken INK:

Bear Forest or Bear World

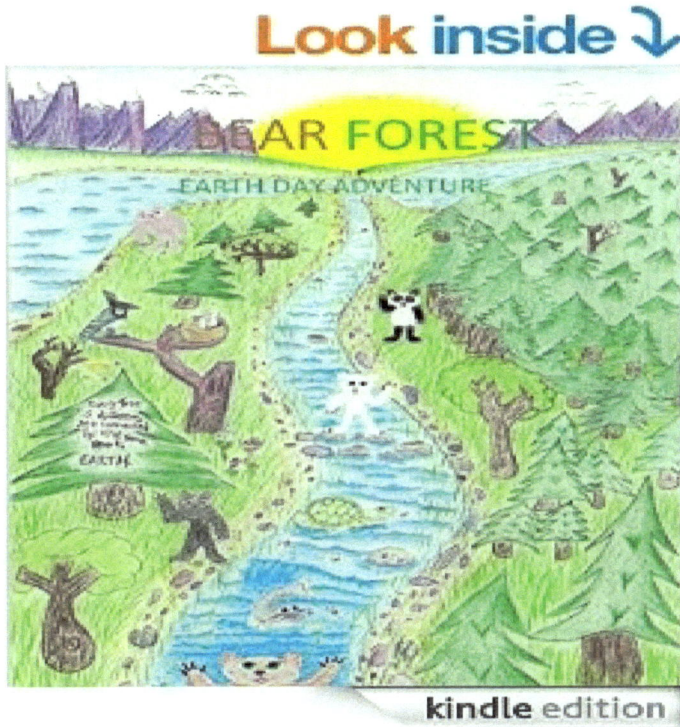

*Now on Amazon.com /.ca

"All life grows up from the same root ... earth. We are all in this together."

Bear World takes place on Earth Day. It's about plotting a better future by giving the unique gifts we give best; and thereby greater our community. A wonderful book to grow up with!

"An uplifting, imaginative, educational story for all ages!"
FOR EVERY BOOK SOLD AN OAK TREE IS PLANTED!

STARLIGHTS AND
SNOWFLAKES

A CHILDRENS BOOK BASED
ON THE LAW OF ATTRACTION

A SELF-HELP Book
For Kids and Adults

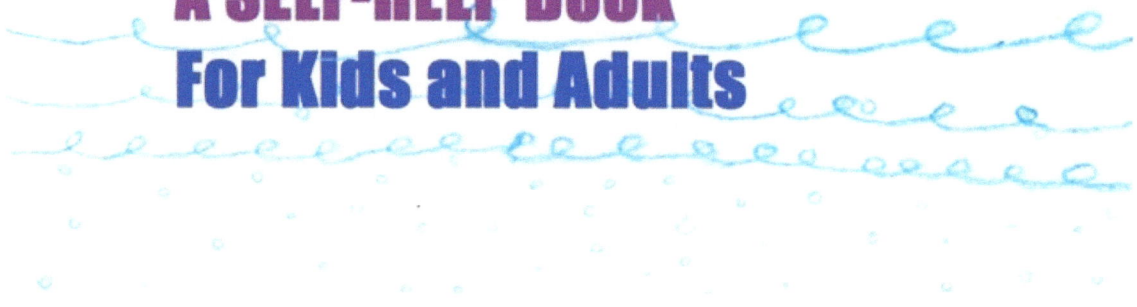

Starlight

Art and Writing
By Nuclear Eyes

Copyright © 2013 by Nuclear Eyes

Second Edition – July 2014

©AWAKENINK

Starlight

ISBN 978-0-9936965-8-9

By Nuclear Eyes

Awaken INK

The Book   of Life

CONTENTS

*A Self Help Book

*For Kids & Adults

ON THE LAW OF *ATTRACTION
AND RULE OF *VIBRATION

Starlight

A POETIC INTRODUCTION:

*Star bright*Starlight, The First star I see tonight, give a guiding invite; for the All-stars insight, revealing Heavenly flights; uplifting spirts to reach new heights.

Let the secrets of time, in starry sublime, ignite, insights, tonight.

Let us absorb, the wisdom, of Starlight*

Author's Note:

This story started as a bedtime story I made up while my 6-year-old daughter was falling asleep. Thank you sweet daughter of mine, who inspired the writing, drawing, and telling of Starlight.

Scene 1: THE SKY

*High in the sky, far above Earth, glowed three stars, in a constellation. One shone as a giant brilliant star, one sparkled as tiny baby star, and the other star spiraled as a faint dim star. As baby star looked at all the stars around him. He was glowing *curious. . .

"Hi giant Brilliant star!" spoke the Baby Star.

"It's always a good day" said the Brilliant Star. "How's light?"

"Light is good, thanks for asking. Can I ask you a question? My dear closest Role-Model."

"Ask a way. Questions are great, because they lead us to knowledge! We can go absolutely anywhere! By asking the right questions, following the right directions, we get from what we are to where we want to be."

"You're so bright! I love questions. So why is that dim Star across from us so faint? How come he isn't bright and shiny, like you are?"

"Well, you see little Sun. It's all about what you're ((emitting)). It's about the message you are *frequently giving*."

"Huh? What do you mean "frequently giving?" You mean, the kind of energy you're emitting?""

"Bright you are! Yes, my Sun. One of the greatest gifts of life is giving. We must give most what we want to come back around. This is how we can build a Good Fortune for ourselves, and those around us! It is good vibes that makes the galaxies dance!"

"Yes, Yes!" twinkled Baby Star. "I want to be a Big Brilliant Golden Star one day! I want to be valuable; to be a beam of service; showing and awakening others to the way! I want to shine!"

"Magnificently Cosmic! *Remember, wherever your heart is, there too is your treasure. The heart lets us know what mood or feeling we are in. If we are giving love, we are helping others."

Also, remember, Everyone's life is an example of what to do or not to do. Dim Star over there, does not have the 'bright attitude. . .'

"I Am so happy and truly grateful for everything there is to Learn!
Life is Good!"

     "You see little Sun," Spoke the Bright Star. "Dim Star takes allot more than he gives. Dim Star does not give out very many positive emotions. He chooses to complain more rather than praise, name call rather that compliment. Dim Star is not on a very good 'role' if you ask me! I don't want you to get too close to him. It would appear to me he could benefit from better habits. better cycles. Dim Star simply needs to think better thoughts, so he can give better emotions. He needs to "adjust his attitude. When you focus on what is good you are filled with light, when you focus on what is not good, it lowers your mood, and dims your vibration"

"RRRRRRRRRRGH! Life sucks you into a hole! It's not very nice."

"So how is it that you two think you're so brilliant?" Asked Dim Star, in a grumpy tone. "You think you're so bright! Who do you think you are?" Dim Star decided to turn away from the answer. "I don't think you're as good as you think you two think you are! I think you guys should give me more! It not my fault I'm so poor!"

"You see," beaconed Brilliant Star "Whenever I talk to Dim Star, I can tell he is angry allot of the time, afraid allot of the time, sad allot of the time. Dim Star also gets jealous of what the others stars are giving; judging, or causing mischief rather than focusing on what special gifts he has to give the worlds."

"I see," said Baby Star. "I sure don't want to be a Dim Star. It's either sad or mad. I want to be glad, I want to be rad! I want to ignite a great sight, as a passionate, courageous star! I want to live in the now, Glow in the Know! I want to be a brilliant star!"

"Very Good!" Spoke the Brilliant Star. "You, Baby Star, are the total opposite of Dim Star when it comes to the energy you are giving. You are giving good feelings. Dim star is more of a taker. Taker stars don't seem to make friends for a very long time, because they always complain, cry, or get angry too easily. They feed off energy, rather than give it. They're usually sad rather than glad, mad, rather than rad."

"I love Dim Star, but I really wish he would follow the advice I give you, Baby Star. Everyone has so much to give, so much to *shine for. I just want the very best for *All-stars! For every soul has a role, a purpose. Everyone has a Story worth telling, a dream worth believing. A cycle worth turning, a lesson worth learning; a gift worth giving."

"***BE THE LIGHT YOU WISH TO SEE IN THE WORLD**. That way life will not suck, rather you will be giving; and everyone will be receiving the love & light you're ((GIVING))."

"Dim Star can you hear me!?" Spoke Brilliant Star compassionately. "I want to lift up my entire cosmic family!" "Lighten up! I try my best to learn from you, why don't you try learning from me too? I simply want the best for you! I want to be the best; brightest role model I can be! With Light as my witness, I will always aim to help others see!"

"So listen well the both of you. "***The Secret to Living Is Giving***! Rather than give negative emotions like fear, or doubt, I choose to give Love! See Love! Be Love! I aim to radiate courage; giving peace, joy, warmth, happiness; lighting up all the worlds around me! I enjoying nourishing all friends and family! The goal of my soul is to help my family get better and better; *to help everyone shine a bit brighter every day!"

"Who do you consider your family?" Wondered Baby Star curiously.

"My family is all Light! All Life! I am the entire Universe, and the Universe is in every heart. I see everyone as an aspect of me. There is no one I would not give my light. Everyone was created for a reason; each Sun has a purpose. So I say *"Good Vibes all around*!" I wish everyone well! I happily give my best to everyone. The more I uplift others, all the stronger, bolder, more brilliant I become!"

"O yes, O yes! I want to become a Gigantic Galactic Giving Star One day!" cheered Baby Star. "I want to glow up to be big and bright like you!"

The Brilliant Star lit up all the more. "The Secret to living is giving. The more you start, the greater your Art. The more you give, the greater you live. You too will become a magnificent star one day. Always remember Little Sun, with sunny raise and starry praise;

((((I LOVE YOU))))!

*There Are 7 Basic Emotions We All Can "*Emit"
((((*Give))))

"Ask yourself little Sun, *What emotions do you feel mostly throughout your day? The majority of your emotions you give throughout the day is how others will see you. . .

*Love

Gratitude*

Joy

Satisfaction:
The Border-line (between + and -)
Sadness
Anger

Fear

Scene 2: **THE CLOUDS**

    * Many snowflakes are riding a cloud on top of the world. They are, star gazing; absorbing the heavenly view. Absorbing the light, and planning their flight, ready to renew the life bellow.

    One snowflake was admiring a larger multicolored greatly-shaped rainbow snowflake, who showed to be truly beautiful from the inside-out.

    "How did this shinny snowflake have get so many extraordinary shapes and beautiful colors?" Thought a curious small snowflake. . .

    "Excuse me Rainbow Colored Snowflake?" asked the curious one.

    "Yes. Great day! How are you?"

    "I'm all light... I was just wondering. How have you gained so many shapes? I have never seen another snowflake with so many colors, with so much outstanding crystal geometry! Oh! You must be a really smart snowflake! I am just wondering... *Can any character get in shape like you?"*

"O You're not ordinary friend! In fact, everyone one of us are very special. At your core you are quite extraordinary. Everybody has the right to create an outstanding path. Each of us is a unique character complete with their own life story and soul journey.

Here is my secret. Every time I land on Earth I simply try to nourish everything I touch. I always aim to leave every creature I meet feel better than when I found them. I aim to make each path better than when I first arrived.

Every new creature I encounter, is a unique design I learn from. These encounters with other forms of life; add to what I know, builds my integrity, and shapes who I am."

"Wow! Now whenever I travel down to Earth, I will always do my best to learn something new! So I can help shape-up everyone I meet along the way, until I return above the Earth a+gain!"

"That's the way little Snowflake. Every day I try to be better than the water molecule I was yesterday! If I do remember to keep a new lesson learned inside of me, I gain a new geometrical shape. This way I increase my wisdom, and build the *character I am."*

"I see," said the watchful little snowflake; absorbing the message the rainbow snowflake was giving.

"Do you mind if I follow you around for a bit? It sounds like I can learn allot from you!"

"Yes of course my friend! Follow my lead until you can lead yourself."

"Great! Let's go gain some new shapes!"

$$\star \; *$$

"Remember little Snowflake. When encountering any creatures, aim to nourish everything you touch. The best way to do this, is when you are about to encounter something new, quietly say inside yourself, "I Love You." The more grateful you are for something, the more you understand that something! Behold, this is the message of the stars! *The Universe Loves Gratitude*!

*I am grateful for every journey; from Earth to cloud. Every day there is something new to observe, learn, and enjoy.

"I love this universe of never ending stories!" Announced the little snowflake. "Life is a play. Everyone is a star character with something to show! Everyone has a unique gift to give!"

Scene 3: **THE CUPS**

*With that, the two new friends began free falling together lightly, for the Earth, excited for another new adventure.

*The Rainbow Snowflake turned and danced, riding the wind. His new friend followed his dance moves, until he felt confident enough to make his own dance.

For nearly an hour they danced in the sky, until the two snowflakes chose the landing spots destined for their path. Both snowflakes picked a warm place to touch down, joining millions of other water molecules in a warm chocolatey whirlpool of togetherness.

**Each snowflake landing in a separate cup of hot fresh cocoa, made with all natural ingredients; a father and daughter were drinking.

Each cup reflected the spiral of the Milky Way Galaxy. The cup filled with spherical bubbles, and the galaxy filled with circulating stars.

As Above, So Bellow.

"The First Snowfall of the season!" announced Father. "Beautiful aren't they? Like people, each one of those snowflakes are different. Everyone is special. Each snowflake has a different path that has developed the unique perspective that has shaped who they are."

The father and daughter looked through the one small opening through the clouds; revealing the stars. All around this natural window; snowflakes could be viewed ridding the wispy winds down to the still Earth.

"They're all lovely in their own special way." The Daughter took a tasty sip of her warm hot chocolate the little snowflake had landed in . . .

"I want to grow up to be a teacher and speaker like you one-day Daddy! I'm curious. . . How can I help others learn to grow big, strong, and smart like you?"

"Good question Dearest. Being a teacher is not just about growing big, strong, and smart. Being a good teacher is about being a good person. Treating others with kindness, leaving everyone you meet feeling better than when you first found them. Remember, growth isn't just on the outside. Growing inside is what counts first and foremost.

In order to be like a star or snowflake, remember you are different. Hold onto what is special bout you. Every eye sees the light of life their own way, just as every star and soul has a unique hue or ray. Everyone has a unique signature. Find what your gift is, and give it out as much as possible! The most brilliant people know how to give from the heart. They let their Core WHY guide their life story."

"We are all made of stardust, snowflakes, and SOUL-OUR-POWER!" Laughed Daughter.

"How bright you are!" Laughed the Father. *"As pieces of the Universe; *We're All Stars!"*

*Love is a Cycle: To Always Be Continued...

"Great attitude of gratitude Dad!
Cheers! Too star lights and snowflakes!"

"Cheers dear Daughter! To Love & Gratitude!"

Starlight

Nuclear Eyes: Look for us On
Amazon.ca or Amazon.com

By Writing a Review on Amazon you can help spread our Message: to Awaken the peek potential in people everywhere! Has any of these stories or their characters impacted your life?

*Let us know how we can improve our service to Humanity.

*To Buy a digital eBook or soft cover copies, please visit amazon and search by author title and name "Corey Marques" or "Nuclear Eyes."

Books For Elder Readers:

⇨ **The Water Bearer**
⇨ (Play& Novel)
⇨ **I AM Light Being Love**
⇨ (Self-Help)
⇨ **A New Planet**
  (Science Fiction)

To checkout or signup for Creative Writing Workshops such as: *The Brainstorm Tree Mind Map, *How to Write a Book*, *How to Ace Create Space, or see when other workshops will be presented by Nuclear Eyes, Corey Marques, Katy Gill, or other Toronto writers and artists; or to see when they will be conducting book signings; you can check the links bellow.

Come see what AwakenINK's Educational Books have to GIVE!

Like & Visit "Awaken INK" on Facebook, or Visit Our Blog and Website:

https://awakeninkorg.wordpress.com

Awaken INK

AwkenINK. Helping People Think With INK.

The Water Bearer: Essence of Love and Gratitude

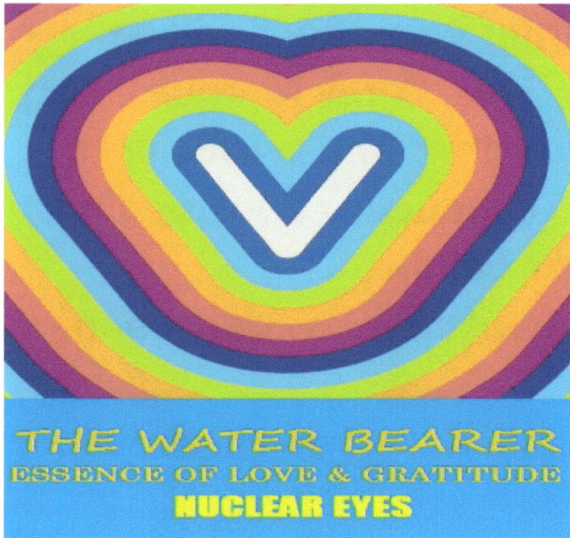

THE WATER BEARER
ESSENCE OF LOVE & GRATITUDE
NUCLEAR EYES

Beholding Water's Mystery (For Adults)

"This book is Rhonda Byrne's The Secret meets Paulo Coelho's The Alchemist."–Winston Woodrich

*Telling someone they are *influential* is the highest compliment. Water conquers mountains every day, so can we."

+ **"The ability you have to affect others, is the most valuable currency there is." –Jim Carrey**

A Novel/Documentary/ Play/

An ambitious cyber journalist and news reporter, *William* sets out on a vision quest to create the Water Documentary of this Century. Little does William know his intention could set the stage for an adventure that may alter the course of humanity's collective consciousness (for the better).

William decides to seek out and interview a legendary character only known as the *Water Bearer*, a mysterious medicine man living in the British Colombian wilderness. On his way to meet the wise Shaman, William comes across a Sea Captain, a Marine Biologist, a Quantum Physicist, and discovers their unique prized perspectives on water.

Everything from taking pictures of water crystals to the

Bear World & Bear Forest

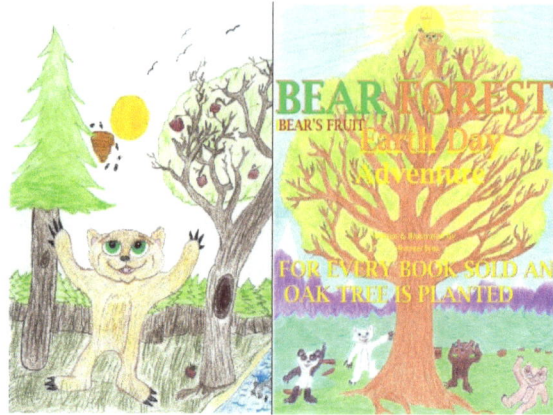

Type "Bear Forest: Earth Day" on Amazon.com to purshase one of the world's very best multicultural books on saving the environment!   (Kids+Adults)

When Gary Grizley doesn't want to clean up the forest on Earth Day, he is shown the bigger picture; how every root is connected to the same Earth.

*For every book sold an Oak Tree is planted.

*You can expand our message by giving us An accurate book review on Amazon.com

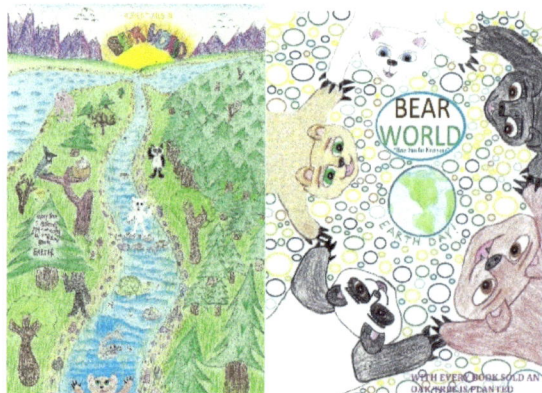

*

https://awakeninkorg.wordpress.com/